Adventures of The Minor Poet

DAVID STARKEY

POEMS

Adventures of the Minor Poet

ARTAMO PRESS

SANTA BARBARA · CALIFORNIA

Published by
ARTAMO PRESS

First published by I*D Books, 1994
First Artamo Press edition, 2007
Copyright © 2007 by David Starkey

Permissions acknowledgements appear on page 5.

Artamo Press is a division of Artamo LLC.

Book and cover design by Jack N. Mohr

Library of Congress Control Number: 2006936690
ISBN-13: 978-0-9788475-3-1
ISBN-10: 0-9788475-3-9

www.artamopress.com

Printed on acid-free paper in the United States of America

ACKNOWLEDGMENTS

Grateful acknowledgment is made to the editors of the following periodicals, where some of the poems in this volume appeared, often in slightly different versions and with different titles: *American Scholar, Ars Interpres, Art/Life, Atomicpetals, Birmingham Poetry Review, A Carolina Literary Companion, Coe Review, Drop Forge, Drunken Boat, failbetter, The Gamut, Grasslands Review, Hampden-Sydney Poetry Review, The Independent, Ink Pot, The Journal, National Forum, Nieve Roja Review, Panic Attack, Poem, Poetry New Zealand, Rattle, Red Wheelbarrow, River City, Open City, Oxford Magazine, Slant, Slow Dancer, South Dakota Review, South Florida Poetry Review, Quercus Review, Switched-on Gutenberg, Trestle Creek Review, Tundra,* and *Whole Notes.*

A number of the poems — again, often with different titles — have also been reprinted in anthologies: "The Minor Poet Buys a Cheese Log" appeared in *O Taste and See: Food Poems,* edited by David Lee Garrison and Terry Hermsen (BOTTOM DOG PRESS, 2003). "The Minor Poet's Poem to Beer" appeared in *Mischief, Caprice, and Other Poetic Strategies,* edited by Terry Wolverton (RED HEN, 2002). "The Minor Poet Doesn't Mind a Little Morning Breath" appeared in *Love Poems,* edited by Oz and Ruth Kraus (BRICK ROW PRESS, 2001). "The Minor Poet Issues Instructions for Composing a Haiku," "The Year His Poetry Became a Fad," and "An Elderly Woman Falls Asleep at a Poetry Reading" appeared in *In Praise of Pedagogy,* edited by Wendy Bishop and David Starkey (CALENDAR ISLANDS, 2000). "The Minor Poet Issues Instructions for Composing a Haiku" also appeared in *The 1995/96 Anthology of*

Magazine Verse and Yearbook of American Poetry, edited by Alan F. Pater (MONITOR, 1996). "The Minor Poet to His Predecessors" appeared in *45/96: The Ninety Six Anthology of South Carolina Poetry,* edited by Gilbert Allen and William Rogers (NINETY-SIX PRESS, 1994).

Author's Note: *Adventures of the Minor Poet* was originally published in 1994 by I*D BOOKS of Connah's Quay, North Wales. I remain grateful to editor Clive Hopwood for his support of the first edition.

However, the book has been out-of-print for some years now, and, with the benefit of hindsight, I have thought fit to include fewer than half the poems from the original volume in this new version.

I would remind readers that the Minor Poet is an invented character, and *Adventures of the Minor Poet* is a work of fiction. Any resemblance to persons living or dead is unintentional and purely coincidental.

CONTENTS

For all the minor poets everywhere,
mutato nomine de te fabula narratur

The Distressed Poet

— after the engraving by Hogarth

Because the pox-faced landlady stands
at the open door harping for the rent,
the scrawny dog snaps at the last
uneaten chop, the bony cat nurses
her frail litter while nestled in the great
coat flung upon the floor, and under-
clothes dry on a line in front of the fire,

because his wife mends her tattered dress
as his only child, ill, wawls in the only bed,
while a few streaks of sunlight seep
into the room of cracked ceilings and walls,
empty cupboards, an empty beer stein tipped
on its side, and reams of wadded paper
scattered across the wintry floor,

because of all of this, I say, not despite,
the poet is able to sit in his dressing gown,
leisurely scratch his head, regard the eight
or ten lines from the previous day's work,
contemplate the substitution of *should
have been* for *might,* then think better of it,
dip the nib of his pen in ink, and write.

The Minor Poet to His Predecessors

O Dora Sigerson, O William Philpot,
O Wilfred Scawen Blunt.

I gospel-chant your names, you minor poets;
Across the pages water-stained,

I celebrate our common bond:
A wisp of genius, genial manners,

Polished numbers we aren't ashamed
To lisp. Blindly in love

With alliteration, sadly moonstruck
By sibilants, devouring whatever

Comes our way, though it is never enough.
Friends: Sackville, Horne, Brighty Rand,

We will remain always anonymous
As grass, as dust, as everything

Needful the world hides in daylight
And open view... Alas! brothers, sisters,

Caroline Elizabeth Sarah Norton,
John Swinnerton Phillimore,

Henry Cust, Richard Jago,
Walter Chalmers Smith.

JEOPARDY FOR CULTURAL ANTHROPOLOGISTS

A. When magnolia leaves sway against the full moon and
   crickets sing softly in bamboo, when night
   advances musky with the scent of grape hyacinth,
   bringing wine and a single candle bright as the Star
   of Bethlehem, this "population" is more likely than
   others to fall in love.

Q. What are minor poets?

Correct.

The Minor Poet Inventories His Grandfather's Tools

"There's a name for everything,"
he said during my childhood

summer visits to southeast Texas.
"You ought to know them all." Out back

in his shop behind the garage
he'd point to the neatly labeled

instruments hanging on the wall:
Wirecutters, Spokeshave, Putty Knife.

The floor was scuffed with grease
but each chipped drill bit had its place.

His world, so self-contained,
incensed my grandmother and she'd show it

by repeatedly flicking the switch
he'd rigged indoors for her convenience.

As he studied the burning end
of his Winston, a squirrel

would pause on a low pecan branch,
or the locusts would shriek

to a crescendo and he'd reach
and gently hand me an Allen wrench

or a pair of pliers or a trowel,
the bulb overhead flashing

like heat lightning from the Gulf.
When he finally chose to squeeze

the padlock shut, I'd look back
through the barred window at twilight

shadowing the wall of wood and steel.

The Minor Poet Remembers Afternoons with His Aunt

When Mother left to play
her weekly game of bridge,
my aunt would sit me on the couch
and lecture on her passion.
Her breath vinous, teeth red,
she'd try to explain syncope
or metathesis. She was dreadfully
serious, though I was only nine,
practically pre-linguistic, had never
lost a medial vowel, had no desire
to transpose my phonemes.
What *did* she want me to do?
The answer, of course, was
listen. It's what I learned from her
about adults, their frightening
need for audience. And once
I realized listening didn't mean
understanding, or even caring
what was said, I let the sounds wash
over me the way she washed down
water glasses of Cabernet:
monophthongization,
regressive assimilation,
epenthesis. *Did you have
a good time, sweetheart?* Mother
would ask, driving me home,
her own slurred speech full
of foreign terms — *doubleton,*

trump and *void* — and I would nod
dumbly, knowing it didn't matter
if I didn't grasp a word.

THE MINOR POET ON OPENING DAY

In the furthest corner of a milo field, I crouch
beside a rotting post. Half-mile away,
my father takes a shot. Trembling, I watch
the sky, and soon a crippled smudge of gray
is in my sights. One blast. I mark the bird
and scale the barbed-wire fence. The purple eyes
blink tranquilly, but those dull eyes are blurred
with blood, the heart pounds fast. Three tiny cries
escape the broken beak. Sharp smell of tar
from turkey mullein. Plash of dark and cold
well water. Smoke on the September sun.
"Home, bud," my father calls, heading for the car.
I'm ten years old: I do what I've been told.
I break the feathered neck against my gun.

THE MINOR POET CHECKS HIS CREDIT

Cleaning the monster car
that passed from him to me,
I found a charge slip
between the seats,
dated 1970.

I hardly knew my mother's father.
He had a stroke when I was eight.
And when I'd visit
once a year,
he'd mumble in his sleep.

The bill lies on my desk,
no use to anyone:
surely it was paid in full
(or presumed missing)
long ago.

Interlude:
An Interview with the Minor Poet, Part 1

INTERVIEWER

So, tell me: are poets made or born?

THE MINOR POET

Excuse me?

INTERVIEWER

You know, is there some genetic inclination toward poetry, some predisposed facility with language, or do poets become poets in response to the circumstances of their lives?

THE MINOR POET

Both. I guess.

[*Silence*]

INTERVIEWER

Nothing else?

[*The Minor Poet shrugs*]

INTERVIEWER

Who were some of your early influences? Shakespeare? Wordsworth? Pope? I certainly hear an echo of both Lowell and O'Hara from time to time — an odd combination, to be sure.

THE MINOR POET

Actually, my early influences were the Sex Pistols and The Clash. Oh, and The Dead Boys.

INTERVIEWER

Nevertheless, you do evidently see yourself in a long line of minor poets?

THE MINOR POET

Literary history makes it clear that most poets are minor poets, like it or not.

INTERVIEWER

And yet "most poets" don't seem especially eager to concede that fact.

THE MINOR POET

That's their issue, not mine.

Traveling, one always returns
With more than one
Set out for. Collecting, when it's begun,
Becomes the *raison d'être,* the sole *epergne*
Of wanderlust. Some pillage gauds
Of native goods, picture ashtrays
Or funny hats. Others take home new gods
When customary faiths have gone astray.
Myself, an inward-looking sort of crook,
I never come back without a stack of books.

I missed the Alps to learn the fate
Of Little Dorrit;
Hearing of a good book shop, searching for it,
I walked right through the most famous York gate.
Old Rome could rise and fall, for all
I cared — I was deep in Cicero.
When Voss was lost, going out of his skull
Outback, outback I was lost in *Voss.* The low
Welsh hills, where I lived a year, are capped with fog,
But I recall the words of the artist/dog.

"Should we have stayed at home...?" Oh yes,
I *do* wonder.
In Norway, the Torrid Zone or Down-Under,
The number of sights I missed you'll have to guess.
But the world, it seems to me, is made
Of fictions anyway. Truly,
The strangeness of Japan's empire must fade

Beside the fiery world of *Kinkakuji*.
From foreign pages I chose each souvenir:
Hiking Kent downs, my face stuck in King Lear.

THE MINOR POET RETURNS FROM THE ORIENT

I was looking for a job
in America.
I was Master of Fine Arts.
I was master of the past
but not the present.

I was sitting on the disabled person's toilet
in a Skipper's Seafood Restaurant.
The smell of whitefish and scallops
mingled with the smell of shit
from my tattered guts.

I was in it.
I was back in it.

In Three Stanzas of Highly Imperfect *Ottava Rima*, the Minor Poet Confronts the Afterbirth of Tragedy

"Tomorrow and tomorrow," laments Mr. Howell...
He thinks he's lost his fortune, although
Every menace there on Gilligan's Isle
Is overcome as easily as Ginger sews
Sequins back onto Lovey's gorilla-ravaged gown,
As simply as the millionaire learns poverty's woe
Belongs to a hapless *Powell*, not his lucky self.
Our castaways toast the happy couple's health.

"Tomorrow and tomorrow and tomorrow," moans Macbeth.
His greedy wife has gone bitchily to hell,
And he fears not just she will be scared to death.
Birnam wood, he finds, is in the wrong dell;
He's vanquished by a foe with stolen breath.
Can you blame his last ironic, "Gee, that's swell"?
Not even an Elizabethan Professor's guile
Could save this king's head from his own wile.

Tomorrow spins up again, but I won't play.
My Fate mutters that any better life
I choose to lead will fast become so fey
That last minute news about my good or bad wife
Will only confirm — not in the least waylay —
Whatever gash is in store from the Scribbler's knife.
Nothing can harm us, nothing set us free:
We're all lost together, Mr. Howell, Macbeth, and me.

THE MINOR POET GETS A JOB

Perhaps the salty air
From the sea not far away
Washes away the acridity
Of bus exhaust and sweatshop smoke…

But not for long.
At work, new tar in the parking lot
Bakes in the arid heat.
Jacarandas drop their blooms.
On the elevator ride up, the scent
Of shoe polish and sweet cologne.

*

My fingers bewitched by caffeine,
I conjure corpses on my screen:
Delete their lives. I am obscene.

*

Each day, a victim of voodoo,
I plunge into
A trance.
And watch
The numbers' dance.

*

Usually we walk to local delis
And feast on tacos, fries, gyros or chow mein.
However, when profits rise, the brass buys us
Lunch somewhere we could not otherwise afford.
Then, lotus-eaters, we taste the herbs of bliss.
Our eyes tear from the onions in *Escalope*

De Veau Orloff. Tongues bathe in the thyme-tinged sauce
of fresh *Cod à la Portugaise.* We're raving
Drunk on two teaspoons of brandy in the heart
Of some dessert. Our bosses sip Perrier,
Assured the money — *their* money — still has friends.
Next month, when we grouse or tire, they'll cast the spell:
Hugo's, Perino's, Pacific Dining Car.

*

The Chairman stalks out with a frown.
My boss gives me a sharp thumbs-down.
I curse a clerk. On down, on down.

*

"Claims. May I help you?"

"Yes, please. I…"

"Check's in the mail
You've reached the wrong division
He's out
I'll have to call you back
I'll have to find your file
We've lost your file
That department was just eliminated
Sorry but we're closed
Try again tomorrow
And have a pleasant day."

*

The day is through. I have a drink
And park myself where I won't think
Of all the nasty things I've done.
Nor all the things still left undone.

The Minor Poet Watches Cable TV with the Ghost of Marianne Moore

Drunk again, I jostle (a little rudely)
the great savant of snails and octopi. She's
engrossed, scribbling notes
    and mumbling remarks

to herself about a herd of black rhinos:
"You never saw them in the circus, just the zoo."
The program through, she yanks
    the remote control

from me, and — quick as a kangaroo rat — jumps
from channel to channel, with comments for each.
Of CBN: "Such eye-
    shadow!" And soft porn:

"I don't need to see what I can imagine
quite well." The Dodgers-Mets game depresses her —
"Where are Gil Hodges and
    Round-Tripper Duke? Blah.

"Los Angeles is no home for baseball."
She takes solace in MTV. Sipping beer,
I watch the hot flash in
    her eyes. The colors,

vivid and changing constantly, draw her in.
"Don't tell," she whispers, as a guitar solo
peals (but of course I will).
    A travel show pans

up the face of Milan's cathedral. "Mother
and I were there — many, many years ago."
This recollection of
    this past seems to tire

the elderly woman. Her eyes aren't as sharp
as they once were. I pat her arm, tell her to
rest and change the station
    to Discovery.

A pit of *fer-de-lances* writhes, as handlers
draw their venom out (the bane effects the cure)
and release them, harmless
    temporarily.

THE MINOR POET BUYS A LIMITED EDITION BOOK OF STAMPS

My neighbor next door glares as he pulls in
from work. I sit here at my typewriter
all day — watching the song sparrows defend
their nests, thumbing my maps — and he is sore
of back from eight hours rolling oil barrels.
He sits on his front steps and cracks a Bud,
glancing at my window between long draughts.
I see resentment rise in him like heat
from the refinery. (He told me once
his father died out there.) Another beer
and he's pointing at me to his wife who nods
and pats his back and gently shuts the door.
He's got a rightful gripe: I'm low by choice,
but where would his three kids be without him?

Led Zeppelin live pounds the thick air: "Rain Song."
He pounds his fist and wipes his face of sweat.
Yes, I'd like to take his family,
entire, on vacation — somewhere cooling,
inside these stamps perhaps. West Quoddy Head
in northeast Maine, at dusk — the trawler full,
the captain smoking in the con, the tower
light swinging round and round. Or Sandy Hook
in a brisk breeze, the ships lined up for New
York's docks. The beaches of Cape Hatteras!
His children would play in the wash, his wife
would read a romance in the shade, and we
would climb the circular staircase and find
ourselves in clean air, lords of the green sea.

But they're only stamps I'm sending off to states
I'm sure he couldn't find to save his life.
"Farewell, Pharos," I whisper to my letters,
a couple Löwenbräus into the heat
myself. And to him: "It was your kind burned
the library at Alexandria."
He can't hear, of course. He's playing softball
with his son, and would no doubt swear he'd never
been near a library. I pause, admit
my fear of everything he knows on his side
of the street. We see each other as across
a stormy strait at night. Two weak beacons
flashing dim warnings ships ignore. He hugs
his little boy. The sky is darkening.

The Minor Poet's Ode to Beer

Like a bee on the tip of my tongue,
its tiny wings buzz.
Already my lids languish,
my inner anvil's muffled in velvet.
The sour smell finds its way
to my throat, cold aluminum
tingles my fingertips.
I taste the Elgar on the radio.

Gerald Locklin, you and I drank warm beer
in the public houses of Hull at noon.
Language, too, hummed
in The Star and Garter,
The Spurn Head Arms. The bitter
filled our mouths with words.
"Right, all right?" the bartender asked
as we stumbled into the bright
fist of afternoon closing time.
But rather than take a dive
we rose like martyrs above the streets.

Beer was our parachute.

Securus judicat orbis terrarum,
said St. Augustine as he conquered
the world with chatter, pious
and sober, the hem
of his robe winking the gold of lager.

The Minor Poet Encounters a Hard Freeze

Now, not just the pipes,
but the people, too,

lie unmoving and exposed.
Across the frigid South,

in attitudes of least
repose, almost all are ice.

The hand of a Montgomery attorney
is welded to the handle

of his Volvo, his child rising
from her car seat is as still as a gazelle

leaping across the veldt
of a Natural History museum.

Grandmothers in Biloxi,
St. Petersburg and Charleston

arch back forever in their rocking chairs,
wishing out towards the sea.

In Memphis, even the pool of Elvis
has truckled to the will of Absolute Zero,

and wreathes of paper roses
bloom a snow-pure white.

Almost all were ice...

and then the sudden, crackling thaw,
Truth scorching my brittle fantasy.
I sliced through the gelid air
to check on my neighbors,
a young woman and her daughter
whom I hadn't seen for days.

Inside, a space heater
had baked their skins powdery
as shaved ice, their eyes glassy
as the frigid surface of a pond.
And I froze there in the hall.
My heart a heap of coals,

I froze.

THE MINOR POET GOES BARGAIN HUNTING
— EVERYTHING IN STORE 60% OFF!!!

Poking among the rows of scavenged shelves,
I feel a song of sympathy rising
for the remaining merchandise.

How painful to be left over on the last day
of business in a bankrupt store.
The bare walls sneer, *Take this junk away!*

Greeting cards with punch lines
that don't work, sweat shirts for schools
that went oh-and-twelve last year, videos

that bombed, tennis trading cards
and bright pink garden hats. I make my way
slowly back into the humid Southern

summer heat, a few offscourings rescued
in my plastic bag: I've felt it, believe me,
that wondering how much, if anything, you're worth.

BUTTONS

For years, I've wanted to write a poem
about the buttons my mother kept in
a 1940s peanut butter jar.
Various, latent with connotation,
just the sort of odd things I tend
to scatter through my verse: some small
as tears, others big as a fifty-cent piece,
inscribed with strange sayings — SPOLIA
OPIMA, EQUIPEMENTS MILITAIRES —
covered with satin or China silk,
black and brown and gray, of course,
but also carmine, maroon and apricot,
sunflower, beryl, pistachio.
Each time my mother dug through the jar
I'd try to fabricate a clever
metaphor, but for years nothing came.
Until today, too late, when I realized
the problem's not the tenor
or the lack of vehicle: the problem
is the poet, who cannot sew.

THE MINOR POET TAKES HIS LEAVE

The wedding is over.
Birdseed scattered across the patio,
bride and groom withdrawn.
A waiter collects glasses
as we sit talking in the August night.

I will miss these pleasant people,
him especially who for months
has not been the friend he once was.
I steady myself against a crepe myrtle branch
before saying good-bye.

THE MINOR POET SETS FREE THE PARAKEETS

Even as I separated their cage
in two, lifted the bars, set the bottom
with its bespattered gravel on the ground
and reached in for the blue-green one,
I knew what I was doing was purely
symbolical. That was precisely
what appealed to me. I liked the thought
that I could move from theory
into practice, could, this once,
conceptualize an event and carry it
through. Bitsy left my hand
and flapped into the bare branches
of the maple tree, like a rook
in some haiku. My breath puffed out
in little clouds. The thermometer
hanging on the back fence read
twenty-three degrees. Bitsy
twisted her head that curious way
parakeets have and fluffed her wings.
I reached in for Molly, the yellow-
green one. She bit my thumb.
I jerked back, cursed, and turned
the bars upside down, shaking until
she flew out squawking, joining
Bitsy in the tree. The dog's
water bowl was covered with ice
and I cracked it with my heel.
Molly leaned over and tapped
Bitsy with her beak, a gesture

of trust and friendliness. The snow
was old and gray, the house
behind them painted brown.
All that expanse of muted color
seemed suddenly to revolve around
my parakeets. I thought of Keats's
nightingale, I thought of Stevens' jar
in Tennessee. But my fingertips
were growing cold. When I went back
inside, they seemed happy enough,
whistling and chirping, singing as recently
freed caged birds are said to do...

THE MINOR POET BUILDS A TOWER OF SKULLS

When I think of Timur the Lame
and his Mongol horde descending on
the Hindu Kush, the hack and slash
of swords, the mortar mixed and poured,
the severed heads — some smashed, others
almost smiling — placed between bricks
by skilled and unprotesting masons,

I conclude that Gandhiji
was wrong, that the human soul
is not a refuge for charity.
I believe then the *Great Chronicle
of 1240,* which judged the average Joe
"brutal and beastly, rather more
a monster than the progeny of God."

Yet just at the moment when
my own skull seems to be untethering,
there comes the memory of crabapples
falling last October: my cracked suburban
sidewalk covered, as though the world
were so bounteous it couldn't help
but give and give and give.

THE MINOR POET BUYS A CHEESE LOG

One week, I decide to buy a cheese log.
Unaccountably, my wife is appalled.
She begs me to buy beer, to buy beef jerky,
to buy Bugles or Godzilla fruit snacks,
anything else. The cheese log is the color
of late pumpkins. Sharp cheddar sprinkled with
sliced almonds. We stand in the aisle arguing
until the prim store manager insists
that we pipe down. But I am implacable.
Finally, my wife admits that the cheese log
reminds her of a former lover, one
I never knew she had. It is like Gretta
and Michael Furey in James Joyce's "The Dead."
Old women stand weeping among the pork chops.
Snow is general throughout the frozen foods.

THE MINOR POET TAKES A JOB AS A DELIVERY MAN

All day I sit in suburban traffic.
Pick-up in Mundelein, drop-off in South
Barrington. Skokie, Western Springs,
Lockport. I bring the goods. My name
is stitched to my uniform, but everyone
calls me Mister. These prairie bedroom towns,
so unnervingly alike, offer, perhaps,
one surprise a day: the charwoman who answers
the door naked, drunk and crying; my gruff
co-worker Don, Union all the way,
showing up one day smelling, unaccountably,
of frangipani. Decembers, I drive
the van so late each road sign begins to look
like the frontispiece of an ancient text.
Hawthorn Woods, Winnetka, Bolingbrook.
Today, I brought a letter to a starlet,
a woman I'd seen several times smiling
in glossy magazines and on TV.
Rap played, sneering and percussive,
as she signed. Hands trembling, she asked
me to wait until she'd finished reading it.
The news, apparently, was bad. She sized
me up, briefly tried a smile, then shut
the door. When it snows, the names come,
unbidden, to my lips: Joliet and Oswego,
Waukegan, North Aurora, Glendale Heights.

THE MINOR POET HITS BLACK ICE

Hard left turn and I kept
turning with the ballet grace
of helplessness. A moment's

carousel. Then my Honda came to rest
on someone's suburban lawn.
Across the street, snow fell softly

on the boxy Church of Christ,
Scientist. The streets were empty.
I couldn't think what else to do

but back up and drive away.
My life is rarely tragic.
I never die (never even leave a skid),

though of course I couldn't help
but understand this must be how it feels,
surrendering control,

forced to look back
at where you've been
as though all the journey lay ahead.

THE MINOR POET SENDS A POSTCARD FROM FINLAND

"What's the Difference Between Turkey and Turku?"
you wrote, facetious as ever. But listen:
not much, really — spelling, the usual
accidents of place. Perhaps the seasons
are worth remarking on, though heat and cold
are twin aspects of the same dynamic.
The *similarities* are what count,
how when you say a name at night it echoes,
the swirl of smoke from street vendors' fires.
Put it this way: in the ancient monuments
of both places there is a smell that permeates
the damp or dusty air, perseverance
and cruelty, as old as the men who built
these ruins, who stacked one brick atop
another in the name of God the creator,
God the destroyer, God the merchant of time.

THE MINOR POET AT THE SUPER SPAR

That first autumn in Finland I finally *felt*
what I'd been teaching for so long: the gap
between signified and signifier,
but also the loveliness of language,
the necessity of our inventions.
It was in the grocery store, among the shrink-
wrapped *parsakaali* and *kukkakaali*,
cruising down the rows of *aamiaismurot*
and *leivoskeksejä*, standing before
the long red slices of *lohi* on ice.
What's important, I thought, is not just
the naming, but also what accretes around
the name, the way flesh covers and swells
over the pit of the sweet, purple *luumu*.

The Minor Poet's Ode to a 500-Gram Bag of Finnish Onions

I've done everything to save you that I could:
put you under the sink, sealed you up
in tupperware, even hung you by a string
out the window — yet still your pungency
is overpowering. In another country
such insistence would be appreciated —
in Italy and Portugal, where kitchens
center houses; in countries where hunger
is a synonym for smell. But here, I fear
the rage to regulate each wayward sense
will make us both unwelcome guests.
So, with this sonnet as your elegy,
I take you to the garbage bin;
let others mourn you by your local name.

The Year His Poetry Became a Fad

It was the coup of a lifetime for a minor poet
like me the day Chuck Brister of Brister,
Schlack & Toille picked up a copy
of *The SoHo Literary Review* (circulation
five hundred plus) in a coffee shop
on the Upper West Side. What he saw
in my poem "Variations on a Phrase
by Kurt Cobain" that ignited his
particular genius for selling things
is for genius alone to explain. I
can only be grateful that, in his words,
"I gulped my latté like it was water
and headed back to the office,
an entire campaign already forming
by the time I left the cab." He found
my number, called. I quickly acquiesced.
The most my verse had ever paid
was a couple hundred contest bucks
and Chuck was talking tens of thousands.
Maybe, he insinuated, a great deal more.

That, of course, turned out to be the case.
The break-through product was the T-shirt
by Hilfiger, which read across the chest:
"Who's to say what seedy script…"
and on back: "Providence will stage
for our benefit?" Then Chanel
brought out Poesis, "A Scent for Men,"
with the tag: "a fragrance as fresh

as his metaphors." The illustrated volume
of my poems (talking point from Chuck:
"Never, *never* refer to it as a comic book")
was such a hit that the movie deal
became inevitable. McDonald's
and Burger King went at each other
for promo rights, but we decided
to go with Taco Bell: the advance
was smaller, but they gave us unheard of
points. I still have the plastic cup
with my smiling caricature and the logo:
"He Claims to Have No Theory
of Fiction at All!" I still sleep
on the Pacific Coast "Enjambment" sheets
and eat off the Minor Poet earthenware,
available exclusively from Pier 1 Imports.

But fads are meant to rage, ransack
and vanish noiselessly. The movie bombed.
In a single fiscal year I was played out.
When it was over, I grew silent,
the way ex-heroes are said to do.
Loathe to go back to the petty
rewards of poetry, the lonely clicking
of fingertips on keys, the unimportant
satisfaction of choosing the proper word,
I invested heavily in risky stocks, and lost.
It was two years before I wrote another line,
and, until today, it's only been occasional
verse: commissioned birthday cards
for CEOs, a "hip" new line for Hallmark

that sold modestly and was dropped.
The moral is obvious, but there's more
to it than that. Money *does* matter.
And when the New American Poet
like me is broke, there's nothing will fix
him up again short of loans so unimaginably
large no mere poet could leverage them.

INTERLUDE:
AN INTERVIEW WITH THE MINOR POET, PART 2

INTERVIEWER

You've bounced around quite a bit. Why is that?

THE MINOR POET

Necessity. Jobs. Restlessness. Who knows?

INTERVIEWER

Has this transience influenced your poetry?

THE MINOR POET

Do you mean has my work suffered from a lack of sustained attention? Have getting and spending, loaning and borrowing, coming and going swallowed up time that might have been more profitably spent writing and revising my poetry?

INTERVIEWER

Yes.

[*Silence*]

INTERVIEWER

You didn't really build a tower of skulls?

THE MINOR POET

No.

INTERVIEWER

Your poetry didn't really become a fad.

THE MINOR POET

No. I made that up.

THE MINOR POET LEAVES THE WRITERS' CONFERENCE IN LOVE WITH SOMEONE (NOT HIS WIFE)

We taxi to the runway; the old woman
next to me grips the armrests. She's talk-
talking to keep from thinking, says, *I haven't flown
in thirty years. But if I remember
correctly, it was like falling in love —
fast and you weren't prepared for it, but
there it was.* She tells me she's going back
to Virginia where it's already late
spring, though here the buds aren't yet on the trees.
Sometimes my heart aches for that place, she says,
then the engines rev and we're hurtling ahead,
the nose tipping skyward, the pavement
giving way, and it's like the first time again,
all thrill and fear, and I say: *I know what you mean.*

Not Having Received an Email from His Beloved in Almost Nineteen Hours, the Minor Poet Writes Another Poem

In that time,
how many crows and sparrows and pigeons,
those dull suburban birds, have come slanting
across the sky, surprised
into cartwheeling, caterwauling love?

How many buds has the wind blown
off the chokecherry tree outside my window?
How many have bloomed?

How many cars have set out west
towards California, cutting through the cornfields
planted now, but far from harvest?

In nineteen hours,
how many times have I imagined you
weighing the steadiness of his bland embrace
against the uncertainty of my mere words,
my fierce desire?

THE MINOR POET CONSIDERS HIS OPTIONS

I sit at the second-story window.
2:15 a.m. Down on
Milwaukee Avenue,
the drunks shuffle home.
Across the street,
a giant flashing sign:
MUEBLES POR MENOS.
An El Train rumbles
towards the Loop. Iron
gates cover the windows
of the hundred furniture stores.
My love, even their facile
come-ons seem like lines
from one of the poems
I spend all night
and day writing you:

NO MONEY DOWN
E-Z TERMS & INSTANT CREDIT
NO REASONABLE OFFER REFUSED

THE MINOR POET HAS FIVE DREAMS INVOLVING A WEDDING DRESS

I   Her divorce was final decades ago,
yet she still stores her wedding dress in a cabin
encircled by heaps of blackberry vines.
Twice a year she revisits her past, parks her truck,
then hikes a path through the woods, drinking
bottles of warm, sweet port, adorning herself
in decaying lace and moth-eaten silk.

II   When she contracts the Shanghai flu
in a San Francisco hotel, she uses
her shabby wedding dress as a blanket,
pulling it to her flushed cheeks. Three
silent days before someone turns the knob.
"Striking," says the manager, a grad student
in Aesthetics at Berkeley, talking
to himself, raising an eyebrow,
passkey still dangling from his hand,
"but is it vulgar or simply inelegant?"

III It is the eve of her golden anniversary.
Her great-grandchildren are sleeping
in the warren of downstairs bedrooms.
Her faceless, perfect husband snores.
She dreams her wedding dress,
exquisitely preserved all these years,
is covered with fire ants, red and writhing.
She wakes with a start, rushes to the walk-in
closet only to find a single black ant,
innocuous, circumnavigating the neckline.

IV   When her husband is away on business,
     she takes the folded wedding dress
     from her grandmother's sturdy trunk
     and glides down the halls of her empty house
     on awkward silk-stockinged feet
     to Tchaikovsky's Greatest Hits —
     dancing with the bodiless gown,
     arms akimbo, everything akimbo.

V   She is in a dressing room, deciding on
     wedding attire. On the other side
     of the thin door her maid of honor jokes
     with the clerk about white or off-white.
     The little room is fragrant
     with new carpet and fresh paint.
     She shuts her eyes, presses the gown —
     soft as crushed velvet — against her face,
     then opens up to a vision of herself bony
     and agéd, stitching a tiny pillow
     with her last saved scrap of shimmering veil.

The Minor Poet Is Awakened by an Alarm

Starting at quarter to six,
the clock radios begin to sound.
The guy above me has one that squawks
like a wounded pterodactyl,
the guy to the right plays classical,
the guy below stays locked
on country-pop. Half the time
I wake early, thinking of you,
thinking of the sadness
of so many single men so close
together, the way we cough
and scratch ourselves and keep on
hitting the snooze buttons,
preferring distant dreams
to morning, postponing
that eventual small summons
of bravery that allows us
to pull back the covers,
find a reason to get up.

The Minor Poet Peruses an Atlas

First day of June and the Midwest
couldn't be further from you.
I sit on the third-story porch
of my short-term apartment
watching lightning flash beneath the clouds.
Traffic sounds. A lone commuter train
from Chicago squeals into its station.
My beer bottle sweats.

I bought a road atlas
at the bookstore tonight.
I needed to calculate the distance
between us. Once,
I would have lingered
over place names, considered
the possibility of side trips
and tourist sights. Now,
it's only the mileage that matters.

As it begins to rain,
I think of the counsel
you must be receiving
against the risks of poetry.

Electricity crackles
fierce and orange across the sky.
Even if it all exploded tomorrow,
no one could tell me
your kiss wasn't worth the heat.

THREE IMMEDIATE NEEDS OF THE MINOR POET:
GAS * FOOD * LODGING

If he asks you how far I'd drive to be with you,
tell your husband three thousand miles. And
no shortcuts, either. Tell him along the way
there would be plains so dry his eyes
would water at the distance, that in Minnesota
they have to haul the dead deer from highways
by the truckload, that every cow in every field
is headed for the slaughterhouse.

If he asks you about the sex, you'd better
tell him the truth — that it matters,
but not the way he thinks. If you want
to give him hope — and everyone deserves
some hope — tell him nothing's certain,
that it's possible to plot an itinerary
and still arrive too early or too late
to stay the night, that most of the exits
are clearly marked "No Services."

But don't diminish the wonder
of what we have, how our two fates
collided the way I-5 and Highway 99 —
the one sleek and fast, the other
a potholed mess — come suddenly together
as the road ascends to Los Angeles.

Last night as I finished my long trip
in the gloaming, cutting from Magic Mountain

to Ventura on 126, I could just see
the oranges hanging heavy in the orchards.
The moon was rising to my left.
Tell your husband I'm with him all the way,
that no sane man who gives his heart to you
should ever want it back.

THE MINOR POET AT THE PILOT HOUSE MOTEL

I   How much do you love me? you asked,
     and I said, Enough to spend a week
     waiting for your visits at the Pilot House Motel.
     We'd been there before, so I knew
     that private planes take off all day and night
     from the airport behind the fence.
     I knew the furniture was cast-off
     mish-mash, that the toilets, like the guests
     were always running, that the carpets
     were bright adultery red and neon blue.

II   When you're not here, I tidy up,
     put the champagne and wine bottles
     in the trash. Afternoons, I swim
     in the pool or sit sunning with a novel.
     I nod at the other visitors — single men
     on unsavory errands, frightened single women
     with their children in tow — and they nod
     reluctantly back. No one asks for names.

III The 4:40 American Eagle for LA
     takes off as I sit down to write this poem.
     Dozens of aircraft are parked
     along the tarmac, but there are no pilots
     at the Pilot House Motel, only passengers —
     and none of us with valid tickets,
     and none of us going anywhere too soon.

The Minor Poet Doesn't Mind a Little Morning Breath

We are so cautious, the two of us,
mornings when we awake — eight
hours of sleep still in our mouths,
the tannin tang of coffee. We are
what we are told to be, polite
considerate of the other's good taste.

Yet I would have us daring, love,
open to the stray sensualities
of real life. Part your lips.
Wider. I want to know every nuance
of your tongue, each moist secret
you can deliver.
                    Let me in.

THE MINOR POET AS BIBLIOPHILE

For months after the divorce, I waited
for my books to show. But when they came,
I hardly read a one. Most sit shut up
now in the garage cabinets I cleaned out
chiefly for the chance to throw away her ex-'s
stuff. Collecting dust. Occasionally,
I dig through them, looking for Hardy or Lowell,
someone I can understand, but they're all shoved
in willy-nilly, and I can't find anything I need.
Sometimes an old contributor's copy will fall
to the grease-stained floor: *The Archer, The Orphic
Lute, Mobius,* or *Smartish Pace* — mouse-
chewed and out-of-print. Sometimes it's only
an old snapshot of my children, left behind.

INTERLUDE:
AN INTERVIEW WITH THE MINOR POET, PART 3

INTERVIEWER

Good God. So, you're a cheater, too? A homewrecker?

[*Silence*]

INTERVIEWER

You abandoned everything for love?

[*Silence*]

INTERVIEWER

[*Sarcastically*] At least you still have your poetry.

An Elderly Woman Falls Asleep at a Poetry Reading

And those of us behind her
can't help but smile.
The forty-something poet
sitting next to me, lately

come to her powers as scribe
of the exotic locale
and significant event,
scribbles a note. "Good poem

for you," she digs,
and it's true. From my vantage,
every minor thing is lyrical:
the lace-trimmed dress

scattered with green roses, red-
dyed hair balding at the part.
Her drooping head recovers mid-
metaphor, then drops again,

the wide pink hat with its nosegay
of plastic roses slipping
from her lap like a sheet
of onionskin. Forty-something

snickers at the snoring.
The poet pauses, gestures
grandly. "And those of us
behind her," I begin.

VANITAS VANITATUM, SAITH THE MINOR POET

In the sunless attic of a used book store
I come upon my secret fear — this tome,
A thousand pages long, of useless, gnome-
Like verse. Above each poem, each proud author's
Photo. Snapshots of ambition: the hauteur
Of a mortgage clerk who knows his rightful home
Is Parnassus (a strident metronome
Accents his dirge). Glaring, resolved — she swore
She'd write — Granny laments the death of her cat.
The dull daily world's thumbed over, remade
In broken prose, prosaically, by schoolboys,
Repairmen, mail carriers — thermostats
Of America. Untrained yet unafraid,
Their off-key voices fill the room with noise.

Defining the Minor Poet: An Essay

The Minor Poet is like a church, an abandoned one,
with a ruined cemetery and swishing
cypress trees.
  The Minor Poet is like a burlap bag
thrown over a "priceless work of art";
the shape of the bag in half-light becomes
itself a work of art; the texture, the smell
of burlap appeal more tumultuously
to the senses than any marbled hall
in all the great museums.
    The Minor Poet is like
a hot shower after a hot bath,
      like smoke
from a teenager's surreptitious cigarette,

like the stolid geometrician who,
unaccountably, decides to deliver
his conference paper wearing wraparound shades.

THE MINOR POET AT THE STUDENT POETRY READING

I realize that poetry is no sport
for middle-age. Two dozen of them, young
and rowdy, and two adults – me and the campus
minister, always working late. Christmas
lights are hung around the windows; coffee
smells and, when the door opens, cigarettes.
The business professors, sensibly,
are all home at ten p.m., while I sit
listening to bongo drums and broken hearts,
the Bosnian refugee who sings a song,
in Bosnian, about a rose. I swear
it is a fickle and cold-blooded art
that can make a grown man weepy-eyed,
convince him half of what he knows is wrong.

The Minor Poet Answers the Question, How Many Poems Can You Write In One Day?

I don't think the question was a taunt,
though with him you can never be sure.
It seemed rather matter-of-fact, like: *How
many times can you make love in one night?*
or: *How long can you run around the block
without passing out?* "I don't know," I replied.
"Do they have to be good?" He shook his head,
no. "Well, ten maybe. Maybe more with coffee
and beer." And then I quoted Stein to him:
*What is poetry and if you can tell me
what poetry is what is prose.* "I asked
you, not her," he said. "All right then," I said,
"I can write fourteen sonnets in one day."
I glared at him. "Just don't expect them to *rhyme*."

THE MINOR POET WRITES TO A FRIEND WHOSE WORK IS MORE SUCCESSFUL THAN HIS OWN

You've always accused me of napping
through my poems — an arrhythmic
somnambulist — even as I tapped
the meter out against my knee. Pale,
with nimbus eyes and a voice
like a clavichord, you fit the advert
better than I. Falcon-instincts
for where and whom to strike
have kept you in the middle
of every hunt. Meanwhile,
I'm the vole who's come up to sniff
fresh air at exactly the wrong time.
I'm the church group leader sitting
around the campfire, strumming my guitar
while you ravish my girlfriend in the pine-
scented shadows. You've outflanked me,
found the counterweight to offset
any pressure I've applied in service
of my career. Another man would claim
you've ruined him, but I refuse —
not nobly, I admit, but out of pride —
to feast any longer on the banquet
of self-doubt you've set for me.
I send you this truce like ransom
in a plain paper bag. Take it, please,
and vanish. The bills aren't marked,
I swear to God; the FBI isn't listening
on the extension, recording every word.

THE MINOR POET ISSUES INSTRUCTIONS FOR COMPOSING A HAIKU

Make it exact: the ribs should show,
firm hoops beneath a thin shield of flesh.
It should sparkle like the skill
of a fastidious artist, precise
as a gnat. It should be a vessel
that requires nothing more than itself
to be full. A footstool. Quick.
A dagger. Microscopic.

Yet make it subdued, as the beginning or conclusion
of a rash. Let it melt
into shade, let it glide *toward* becoming
the way tides suggest something
about the shoreline that would otherwise
go unrecognized.

Granted, brevity and novelty
are its chief merits.
So above all it should shock
like the backward roll of thunder
in an unexpected gale.
                              Worried
they'll see through it,
the knaves and hags? Worried
they'll toss it like dry straw onto a trash fire?
Don't worry: call it a frigate and name it
after a state. Conviction propels.
If they think it's seaworthy,

it'll float,
goddamnit,
it will float.

THE MINOR POET CONSIDERS THE INADEQUACY OF METAPHOR

> How, for instance, thorns
> on the red branches
> of a blackberry bush
> look so much sharper
> when they poke out
> from a "blanket" of snow,
> which, in fact, is neither
> soft nor comforting nor warm.

Fax Mentis Incendium Gloriae

For twenty years now I've been typing
up my poems, sending them out
and getting them back in little magazines.
You'd think that all those well-chosen words
would count for something in the way
of *gloriae*.
      But when I came to London
I wasn't greeted at Heathrow by mobs
of fans and armies of simpering reporters.
The tabloids did not herald my arrival
with three-inch headlines. No limousine
whisked me away to the Berkeley Hotel
or an all-night rave at Zombies Ate My Brain.
My obscenely wealthy friends did not insist
that I be guest of honor at a private
dinner party in their Mayfair mansion.
                                    No,
when I came to London I took the Picadilly Line
and carried my own suitcase from the tube stop
to my two-star hotel. The night clerk
didn't raise an eyebrow as he copied down
the name on my passport — although
when he looked up to check my face
against my photograph, I swear I saw
a glimmer of recognition in his eyes....

THE MINOR POET'S ADVICE TO HIS POETRY STUDENTS ON THE LAST DAY OF CLASS

Distrust advice:
everyone will tell you that.

Better yet, embrace the worst idea
I've thrust upon you.
Lick its ears and sweaty neck.
Take it home to Mom.
Arouse it in your bedroom
then insist on sleeping alone.
At breakfast, say you never
want to see it again,
                              but take it
by the hand when it follows meekly
to the backyard. Tell it the names
of local birds and plants. Show it
where you scraped your knee
when you were learning
how to ride a bike.
                              By this time,
there should be advertisements
for designer scents and underthings
revolving in the sky.
                              Don't look up.
Kick it in the knee, blackjack it
with a sock full of quarters, pile it
in the trunk of Dad's Buick
and drive it into the lake.

Now you can begin again on your own.
I won't be watching.
I promise.

*

Also, don't forget
the first part of this poem.

INTERLUDE:
AN INTERVIEW WITH THE MINOR POET, PART 4

INTERVIEWER

You dispense quite a bit of advice in your poetry.

THE MINOR POET

One can't really help it, can one? I mean, what is poetry if not a kind of advice column in verse?

INTERVIEWER

Do you really believe that?

THE MINOR POET

I don't know. Do you?

INTERVIEWER

Hardly. I believe the reader should be offering advice to the poet, not the other way around.

THE MINOR POET

Are we finished?

INTERVIEWER

Not quite. Is there any philosophy underpinning your poetry?

THE MINOR POET

Despair.

INTERVIEWER

Despair? Is that all? That's not exactly a philosophy.

THE MINOR POET

It can be.

[*Silence*]

INTERVIEWER

It must be difficult, spending your life devoted to a single demanding craft, without ever really reaping the rewards.

THE MINOR POET

What do you mean?

INTERVIEWER

Just ... you're not exactly a household name.

THE MINOR POET

What poet *is* a household name?

INTERVIEWER

Some are closer than others.

THE MINOR POET

Fair enough.

INTERVIEWER

But you're not one of them.

[*Long silence*]

THE MINOR POET

No.

EPILOGUE: THE MINOR POET'S *ARS POETICA*

Visual artists have it made,
I mean *made,* right there in front of them.
They spread paint thick
as cookie dough across a canvas.
They pry rhinestones and glass beads
from costume jewelry, cover a cuckoo clock
with glue and — *Voila!* — their art.
Even if nothing comes
of an afternoon spent gouging
and caressing a wet lump of clay,
they still have the flecks of earth
dried to their face and arms,
the warm water and soap
on their hands.
               But imagine
you are a young black man from Oklahoma
come to New York to play guitar.
Imagine you are Charlie Christian
breathing the smoke of Minton's
into your tubercular lungs, red-hot
and burning out fast,
yet your genius going all but unrecorded.
Your audience sees your fingers moving
across the frets, but there is no accounting
for the proud, gut-stricken slur
coming from your amplifier.
Imagine emptying your life into the invisible.
Willingly.

Now *that* would be something like poetry.